D1681216

ELVIS
THE KING OF ROCK & ROLL

GREER LAWRENCE

TODTRI

Copyright © 1997 by Todtri Productions Limited. All rights reserved. No part of this publication may be reproduced, stored in a retrieval system or transmitted in any form by any means electronic, mechanical, photocopying or otherwise, without first obtaining written permission of the copyright owner.

This book was designed and produced by Todtri Productions Limited
P.O. Box 572, New York, NY 10116-0572 Fax: (212) 279-1241

Printed and bound in Singapore

ISBN 1-57717-021-0

Author: Greer Lawrence

Publisher: Robert M. Tod
Editorial Director: Elizabeth Loonan
Senior Editor: Cynthia Sternau
Project Editor: Ann Kirby
Photo Editor: Edward Douglas
Picture Researchers: Heather Weigel, Laura Wyss
Production Coordinator: Annie Kaufmann
Design and Typesetting: Theresa Izzillo

Elvis and Elvis Presley are registered trademarks of Elvis Presley Enterprises, Inc., which is not associated with the author of this book or with Todtri Productions Ltd, the packager. The work is not licensed, endorsed, or sponsored by Elvis Presley Enterprises, Inc.

Every effort has been made to locate the copyright owners of the material used in this book. Please let us know if an error has been made, and we will make any necessary changes in subsequent printings.

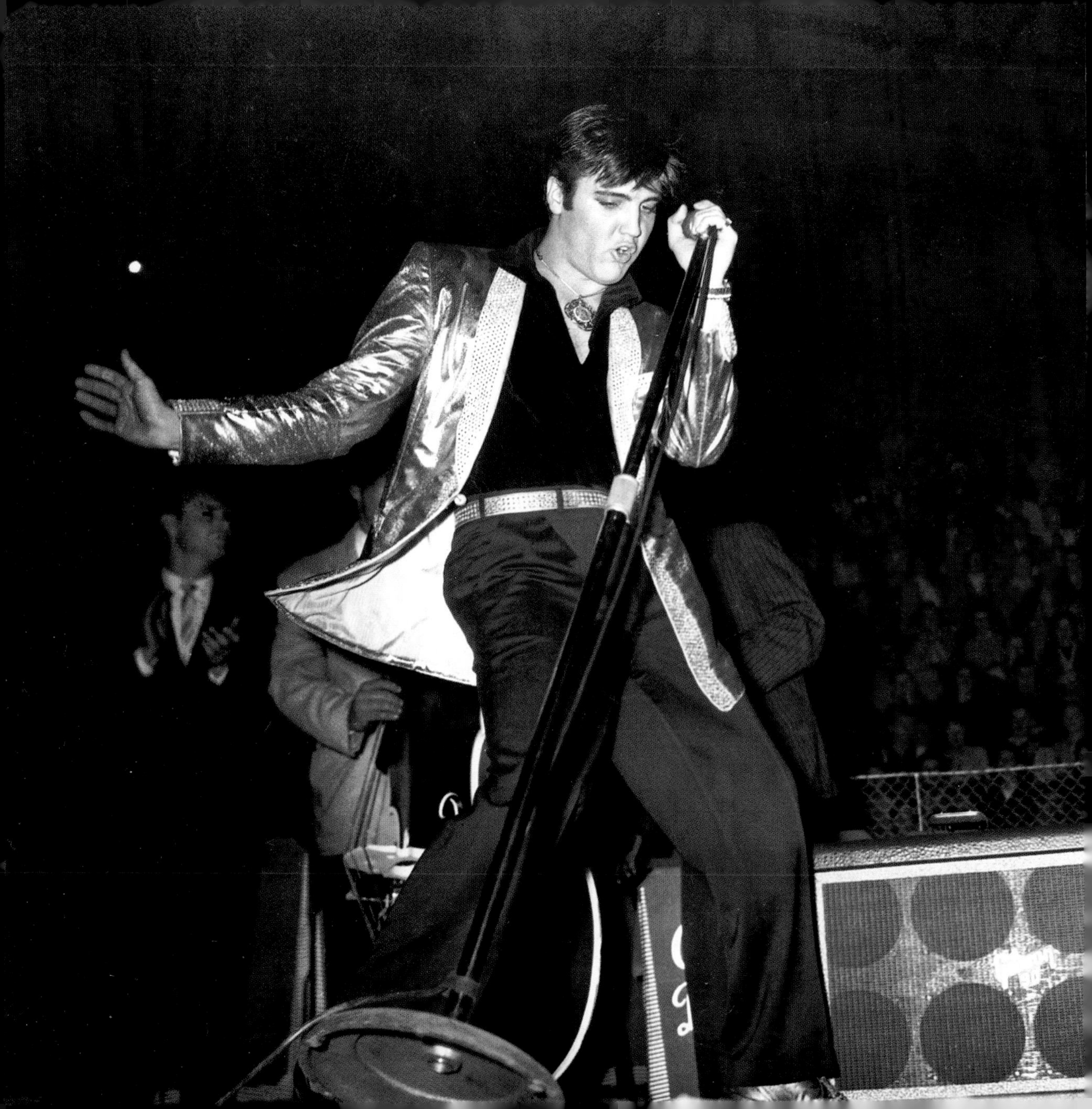

1935

> "Before Elvis, there was nothing."
> — JOHN LENNON

BIRTH

East Tupelo, Mississippi, January 8, 1935: Elvis Aaron Presley was born at home at 4:35 a.m. to Vernon Elvis and Gladys Love Smith Presley of 306 Old Saltillo Road (now 306 Elvis Presley Drive).

Elvis was the second of two twin boys; his brother, Jesse Garon, was stillborn. His parents lived in a two-room shotgun shack built with borrowed money and the help of relatives. The tiny house was often shared with others. But the Presleys were determined that their only child should have a better life—the boy from the wrong side of the tracks was not destined to stay there.

Tupelo, MS

ELVIS: THE KING OF ROCK & ROLL

YOUTH

Elvis was extremely close to his mother, and their relationship remained unchanged until her death. Gladys encouraged his love of church and gospel singing and taught him his impeccable manners. By the time he was nine, Elvis could sing any popular country tune, hymn, or gospel song from memory. He was even hanging out with professionals at WELO, a Tupelo radio station.

But times were tough. When Vernon was able to find work in Memphis in 1948, the small family pulled up stakes. During high school, while all the other boys wore simple clothes and had crew cuts, Elvis emulated the styles popular among the black rhythm-and-blues musicians he saw performing on Beale Street. His classmates taunted him mercilessly, but Elvis stuck to his unique style. Throughout his life, he never forgot where he came from.

Gladys and Vernon pose with their famous son at their home on Audubon Drive.

Gladys

Elvis at age twelve, about a year before the struggling family moved to Memphis.

Firsts

Elvis' Firsts...

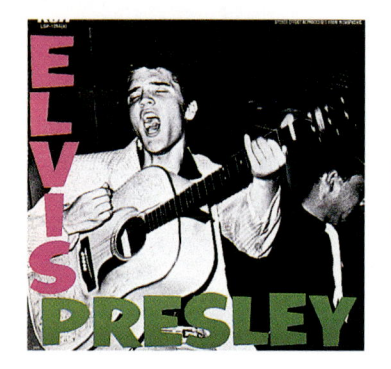

Album: "Elvis Presley," recorded on the RCA label, was released on March 13, 1956. It held the number-one spot on Billboard's pop chart for ten weeks and went gold.

Guitar: For his eleventh birthday, Elvis' mother bought him the most expensive guitar at the Tupelo Hardware Company. It cost $12.95.

Radio Appearance: In 1945, at the age of ten, Elvis sang "Old Shep" in a talent contest held at the Mississippi-Alabama Fair and Dairy Show and broadcast over Tupelo radio station WELO. He won second prize.

good rockin' tonight

Recording: Soon after graduating from high school in 1953, Elvis went to Sun Studio to make a demo. He laid down two tracks—"My Happiness" and "That's When Your Heartaches Begin"—and gave the record to his mother as a belated birthday gift.

Single: Recorded in the wee hours of July 6, 1954 on the Sun label, Arthur Crudup's "That's All Right, Mama" (with "Blue Moon of Kentucky" on the flip side) was Elvis' first single. It aired the next night, becoming an instant hit on local radio stations.

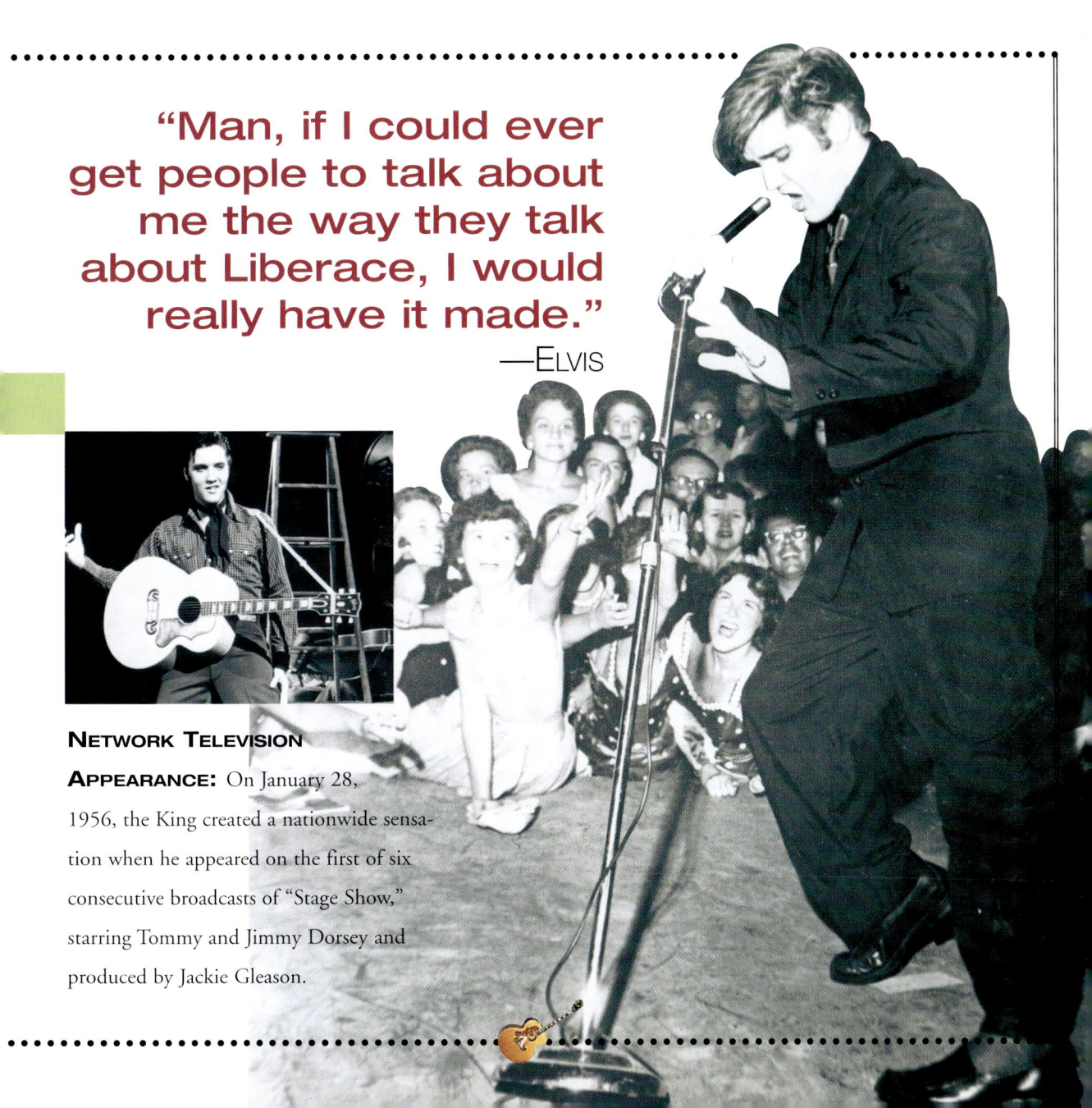

> "Man, if I could ever get people to talk about me the way they talk about Liberace, I would really have it made."
>
> —Elvis

NETWORK TELEVISION APPEARANCE: On January 28, 1956, the King created a nationwide sensation when he appeared on the first of six consecutive broadcasts of "Stage Show," starring Tommy and Jimmy Dorsey and produced by Jackie Gleason.

SUPERNOVA!

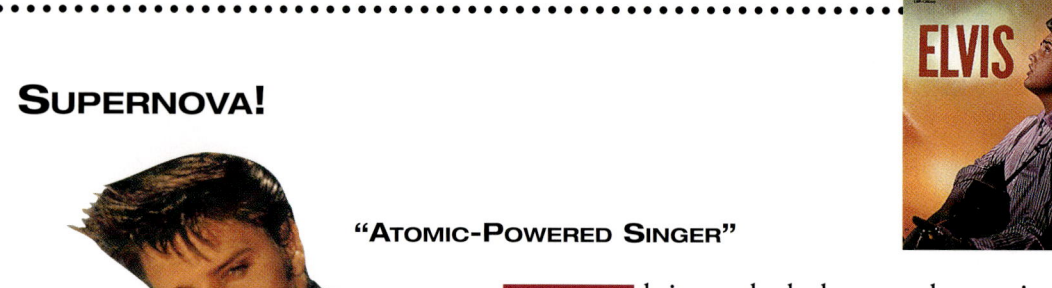

"ATOMIC-POWERED SINGER"

Elvis exploded onto the national scene in January, 1956, when he appeared on TV's "Stage Show," produced by Jackie Gleason. He was an overnight sensation, a phenomenon never witnessed before or since. Teenage girls screamed and swooned while their parents condemned Elvis' "lewd" behavior. Before long, Elvis was a familiar name in every American household, and across Europe, too.

hound dog

Elvis loved cars—big, shiny Cadillacs and Lincolns, high-powered Mercedes-Benzes, stately Rolls-Royces—and he gave them away at the drop of a hat.

ELVIS: THE KING OF ROCK & ROLL

"He can't last. I tell you flatly, he can't last."
—Jackie Gleason

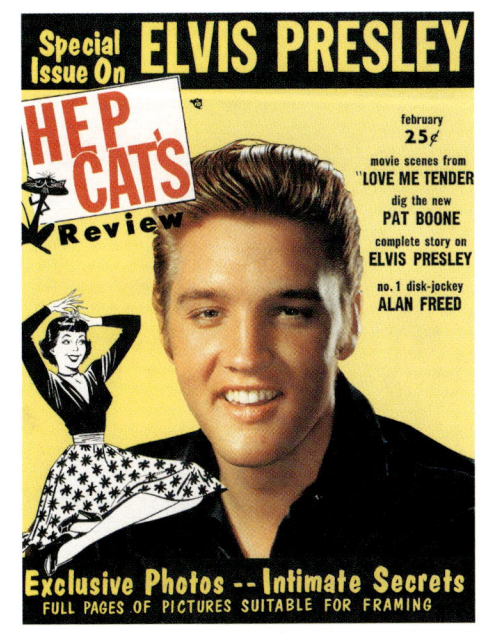

Success

Success followed success. Soon Elvis was touring the country in concert, recording his first album, and being featured on more and more television shows, including Ed Sullivan's popular "Toast of the Town." In an incident that remains notorious to this day, Elvis was shown only from the waist up during his *third* appearance on *The Ed Sullivan* show, but was not censored during the first and second. But this tactic backfired—the emotions of home viewers were stirred even further when they witnessed the hysteria of the studio audience.

Elvis prepares to go live on The Ed Sullivan Show.

Teenage girls screamed for their idol while outraged church and civic leaders, as well as the press, criticized Elvis' public performances.

STAR PROPERTY

Elvis' fans grew more enthusiastic each day. Girls covered his car with messages written in lipstick or scratched their phone numbers into the paint. Crowds often gathered outside his home, hoping to catch a glimpse of him.

HOLLYWOOD

With his star rising, Elvis' next stop was Hollywood. In 1956 he made his big-screen debut in *Love Me Tender*. Despite terrible reviews it was an instant hit, and established him as a major box-office draw.

LOVING YOU

Elvis had his first on-screen kiss in *Loving You*, his second movie, in which he plays an unknown Southern singer in a plot based loosely on his life. He arranged to have his parents with him during the shooting, and Vernon and Gladys even appear in cameo roles. After Gladys' death, though, the King never watched *Loving You* again—seeing his mother on screen was simply too painful.

BAYOU BLITZ

King Creole, Elvis' fourth and best-received film, was shot on location in New Orleans, and it was there that his true stardom became clear to the world. Police

king creole

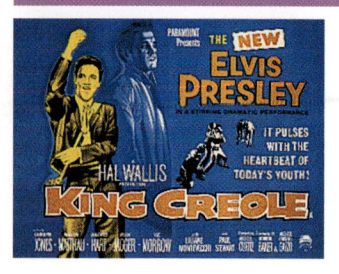

The U.S. draft board granted Elvis a 60-day extension from military service so he could shoot *King Creole*.

were called in to control crowds on the city's streets, and Pinkerton guards were hired to patrol Elvis' hotel, where the King had to climb down a fire escape from the roof just to get to his room. A group of female admirers even held Elvis hostage in an elevator, just to be near their idol. But all the attention had its price, and Elvis was forced into seclusion.

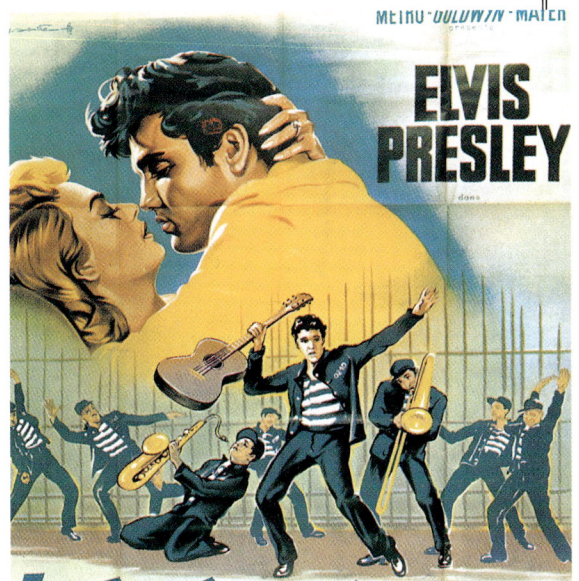

On October 17, 1957, *Jailhouse Rock* (released in France as "le Rock du bagne") premiered in Memphis. Elvis did not attend.

In the Army

March 24, 1958: "Black Monday": Elvis inducted into the U.S. Army, A Company, Second Medium Tank Battalion, Second Armored Division, and reports to Fort Chaffee, Arkansas for indoctrination. Fans grief stricken.

March 25, 1958: Barber James Peterson shears off Elvis' legendary locks. The King quips, "Hair today, gone tomorrow!"

March 28, 1958: Private Elvis Aaron Presley, 53310761, goes to Fort Hood, Texas, for basic training. He calls his mother every night, and fan letters pour in.

August 14, 1958: Gladys Presley dies of a heart attack brought on by hepatitis. Elvis is devastated.

September 22, 1958: Fans at the Military Ocean Terminal in Brooklyn, New York, scream and sob as Elvis boards the ship to take him to his post at Bad Nauheim, Germany. *Photoplay* magazine reports his parting words: "Please don't forget me when I'm gone."

·•· ELVIS: THE KING OF ROCK & ROLL ·•·

Private Presley

NOVEMBER, 1959: Priscilla Beaulieu, age fourteen, daughter of Air Force Captain Joseph Paul Beaulieu, is introduced to the King at an army party in Germany.

MARCH 2, 1960: Elvis flies from Germany to McGuire Air Force Base in New Jersey, is greeted by Nancy Sinatra, bringing him a gift from her father.

MARCH 5, 1960: Sergeant Elvis Aaron Presley honorably discharged from the army at Fort Dix, New Jersey. Fans the world over breath a sigh of relief.

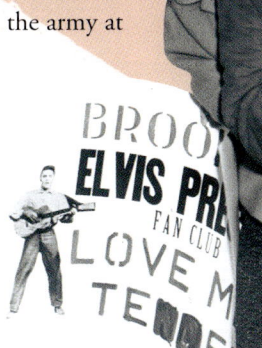

"Elvis Presley is the greatest cultural force in the 20th century."
—Leonard Bernstein

it's now or never

The King and Frank Sinatra exchange quips during the "Frank Sinatra-Timex Special."

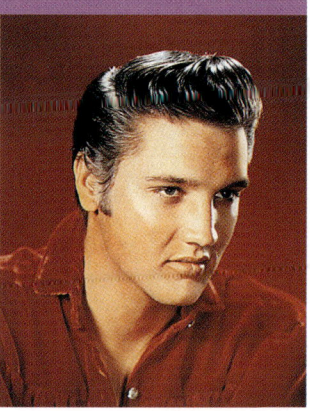

ELVIS IS BACK

AFTER THE ARMY

After a two-year drought while he served his tour of duty in Germany, Elvis' fans were dying for their favorite rocker, and 1960 and '61 brought a whirl of interviews, concerts, TV appearances, movie shoots, and recording sessions. In fact, only two weeks after setting foot on American soil, the King ensconced himself in a Nashville studio to record the album "Elvis Is Back," an immediate best-seller.

Elvis in the recording studio.

HERE TO STAY

It was during these years that Elvis began to gain acceptance among his former critics. With "Elvis Is Back" came a new Elvis—leaner, more mature, without the "rebel" haircut but with as much magnetism as ever. He officially gained the Establishment Seal of Approval on May 8, 1960, when he appeared, tuxedo-clad, on TV's "Frank Sinatra-Timex Special" (also called "Welcome Back Elvis").

Movies! Movies! Movies!

Elvis spent most of his time from 1960 to 1968 making movies, turning them out at the rate of three or four per year. All did well at the box office, though some were bigger hits than others. And most were accompanied by sound-track albums, four of which reached number one on the charts.

What fan wouldn't swoon over this sexy star?

g.i. blues

On August 3, 1959, Paramount announced that *G.I. Blues* would be Elvis' first feature film after the Army.

ELVIS: THE KING OF ROCK & ROLL

Dear Elvis, February 9, 1966

You're movie played 2 weeks at Loew's and I saw it <u>at least</u> twice a day. I can hardly wait to see it again when it comes to the neighborhood. I have seen it 29 times!

return to sender

In *Viva Las Vegas*, Ann-Margret, as Rusty Martin, a hotel swimming instructor, and Elvis, as formula racer Lucky Johnson, dance up a storm during their sultry romance before the Las Vegas Grand Prix.

Lights, Camera, Action!

Flaming Star

While almost all of Elvis' movies from the 1960–68 period were lighthearted musical comedies, he did have a chance to prove his acting abilities in *Flaming Star*. The film was such a hot property that Marlon Brando was originally considered for the lead role, but negotiations fell through and the King was signed for the part.

But even though he gave an admirable performance, *Flaming Star* was a comparative flop. The fans demanded music, and Elvis was disappointed by the public's poor reception.

Aloha Oe

Blue Hawaii was the first of three Presley movies set against the backdrop of the lush scenery of the Aloha State. (Amusingly, thirty-five-year-old Angela Lansbury plays the part of his mother.) In response to the fans' appeals for more music, it contains fourteen songs, including the meltingly romantic "Can't Help Falling in Love With You." Both the song and the film were a tremendous success—the fans had spoken.

girl happy

Kissin' Cousins, a 1963 release from Metro Goldwyn Mayer, opened on March 6. Number 26 on *Variety*'s Weekly List for 1963, the film grossed $2.8 million.

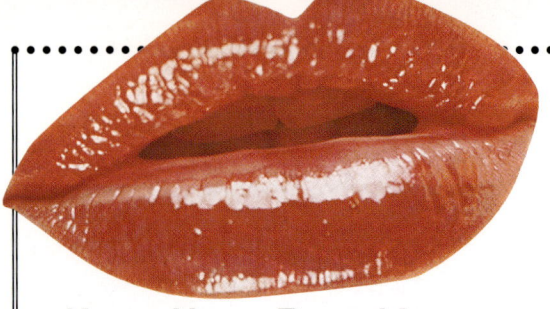

Girl Crazy

Hunka-Hunka Burnin' Love

From the very beginning of his career, girls flung themselves at Elvis wherever he went. And why not? He was gorgeous, sexy, provocative, and hypnotic! The shy boy from Memphis dated up a storm. Beauty queens, movie stars, Vegas showgirls, even receptionists—no woman was immune to the King's considerable charms.

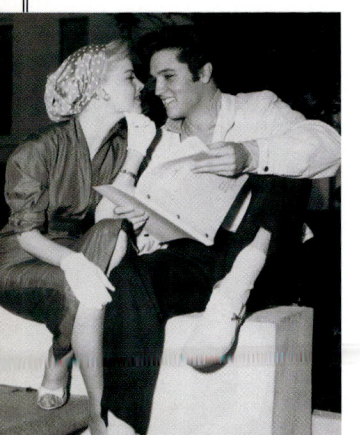

Stuck On You

Elvis' first girlfriend was nine-year-old Caroline Ballard, the daughter of the minister at the East Tupelo First Assembly of God Church; his last was actress Ginger Alden. He dated dozens of beautiful women from co-stars like Ann-Margaret, Juliet Prowse, Nancy Sinatra, and Debra Paget, to stripper Tempest Storm, *Playboy* playmate Sheila Ryan, and voluptuous but very married Mamie Van Doren. Other lucky, well-known love interests included Cybill Shepherd, Rita Moreno, Bobby Gentry, Connie Stevens, and Natalie Wood. But Elvis' heart always belonged to his wife, Priscilla.

Glam Scam

Along with Elvis' reputation for

Actress Yvonne Lime with Elvis at Graceland in 1957.

> "He's just one big hunk of forbidden fruit."
> —Anonymous Female Fan

Whether in film or fact, beautiful women followed Elvis almost everywhere he went.

i got stung

being a ladies' man came a certain amount of wishful thinking on the part of some of his fans. While a number of women have claimed to be secretly married to Elvis or to have borne him a "love child," probably the most outrageous hoax any fan ever perpetrated was the 1976 "wedding" planned by Iladean Tribble of Athens, Alabama. When the announcement of her upcoming marriage to the King was published in a local newspaper, hundreds turned up to witness the non-existent ceremony.

Elvis and Priscilla cut the first slice of their wedding cake.

"Over the years, he became my father, husband, and very nearly God."

—Priscilla Beaulieu Presley

ELVIS: THE KING OF ROCK & ROLL

"LOVE ME TENDER"

THE WEDDING

In a small, private ceremony on May 1, 1967, in Las Vegas, Nevada, Elvis married his longtime sweetheart, Priscilla Ann Beaulieu. The King gave his 'Cilla a three-carat diamond, and she gave her new husband a gold band. The bride wore a white silk organza gown adorned with seed pearls and a six-foot train; Elvis wore black trousers topped with a black brocade jacket and matching vest. At a champagne breakfast reception following the nuptials, roast suckling pig, Southern fried chicken, and oysters Rockefeller were served, as well as a five-foot, six-tier wedding cake!

THE LIGHT OF HIS LIFE

On February 1, 1968, Elvis' daughter, Lisa Marie was born—exactly nine months to the day after the wedding. The King doted on his precious girl, showering her with love and gifts at every opportunity. Tragically, Elvis and Priscilla were divorced in 1973.

DID YOU KNOW? ELVIS' FAVORITE THINGS:

RECORDING ARTISTS: Billy Eckstine, Arthur Crudup, Hank Williams, Mario Lanza, Mahalia Jackson, B.B. King, Tom Jones, Dean Martin, and others

TOY: Teddy bear

SOAP: Neutrogena

AFTERSHAVE: Brut

ACTORS: James Dean, Marlon Brando, Rudolph Valentino

MOVIES: *Patton*, *Dr. Strangelove*, *Monty Python and the Holy Grail*

king cotton

SPORTS: Karate, raquetball, football (Cleveland Browns)

MAGAZINE: *Mad*

COMEDIANS: Peter Sellers, Monty Python

BOOKS: The Bible, *The Prophet* by Kahlil Gibran

BIBLE PASSAGES: I Corinthians 13:1, Matthew 19:24, Psalms 101:1

······ ELVIS: THE KING OF ROCK & ROLL ······

TV Show: "Kung-Fu"
Animal: Tiger
Colors: Black, white, blue, gold, pink
Bacon: King Cotton

"When we were kids, growing up in Liverpool, all we ever wanted to be was Elvis Presley."
—Paul McCartney

No Coke, Pepsi . . .

Elvis was quite a hearty eater, enjoying down-home specialties like pork chops, corn pone, mashed potatoes and gravy, apple pie, Whammies (ice-cream bars), burnt bacon, peanut-butter-and-banana sandwiches, and cheeseburgers. And he preferred to wash it all down with Pepsi.

"If your head gets too big, it'll break your neck." —Elvis

Graceland

Elvis at home, outside of Graceland.

The King's Castle

By 1957, the crowd of fans outside the Presleys Memphis house was too large to handle, and so, in March, Elvis purchased Graceland, which was to be his beloved home and refuge for the rest of his life.

The mansion sits on fourteen acres on the southern edge of Memphis; it is a grand colonial, faced with pink Tennessee fieldstone and an imposing pillared portico and surrounded by an 8-foot stone wall.

The King had his palace renovated and decorated—to the tune of a half-million dollars—in a style as flashy as his stage shows. Over the years, he continued to change the shape and style of his home, but some elements—deep shag carpeting, glittering mirrors, gilt trim, rich reds and purples, thick, sensuous velvet—remained constant.

A National Attraction

Today, Graceland—placed on the National Register of Historic Places in 1991—is one of America's top tourist attractions, visited by as many as a quarter-million people each year. Outside, the pink stone wall, called the "Wall of Love" by fans, is covered with graffiti messages to Elvis.

Elvis' famous gold-plated grand piano, one of the treasures of Graceland, is now on display at the Country Music Hall of Fame in Nashville, Tennessee. Graceland will always be the mecca of Elvis museums, but there are also dozens of other places which house memorabilia and invite visitors. Some are in Memphis—Sun Studio, Taylor's Restaurant (now Sun Studio Cafe), the Memphis Police Museum—while others are scattered around Tennessee, Mississippi (his first home in East Tupelo is open to the public, too), and the rest of the U.S. There are even Elvis museums in England, Canada, and Sweden.

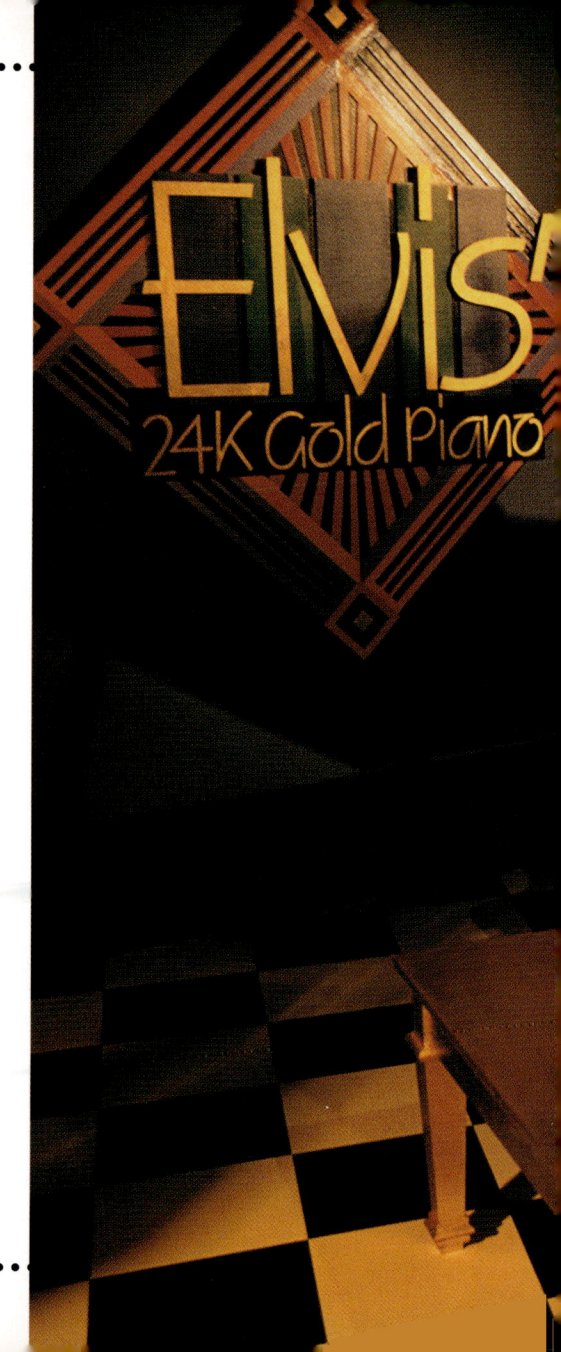

"Life is more than just drawin' breath." —Elvis

No More Movies

Slow Fade

Elvis' last six movies, all released in 1968 and '69, were not his best, and he was the first to admit it. For the most part, these represent a dramatic departure from his earlier, more successful films. There was less music and fewer exotic locales—two elements enormously popular with his fans.

In *Live a Little, Love a Little*, commercial photographer Greg Nolan (Elvis) often finds himself in strange surroundings.

"The only thing that's worse than watchin' a bad movie is bein' in one!"
—Elvis

ELVIS: THE KING OF ROCK & ROLL

CHARRO!

Much to everyone's disappointment, *Charro!* stands out as the King's worst film. It is a straight Western in which Elvis sings only one song, heard during the opening credits. Like *Flaming Star*, *Charro!* was a failed attempt at turning Elvis into a serious leading man, and only added to his growing dissatisfaction with the movie business.

CUT!

Though well received, *Change of Habit* was Elvis' last feature film. Mary Tyler Moore co-stars as a nun who falls in love with a caring, dedicated physician (Elvis). The melodrama ends in a cliffhanger, and the audience is never told whether the Sister chooses her vows or the doctor.

speedway

Stay Away, Joe opened nationally on March 8, 1968, becoming #68 on *Variety*'s list of top grossing films.

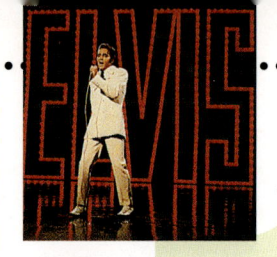

THE COMEBACK SPECIAL

1968 was a banner year for Elvis—not only was his daughter, Lisa Marie, born, but he also made his first television appearance since the 1960 Sinatra special. Officially titled "Singer Presents Elvis," the show came to be known as "The '68 Comeback Special," for the King had not performed before a live audience since 1961. The program, which aired on December 3, was an enormous hit. Elvis looked trim and overwhelmingly handsome in his multi-thousand-dollar wardrobe, and sang with more passion than he had in years. So great was the response that hundreds of thousands of Elvis' records flew out of stores during the following week. The King was back on top once more, and hotter than ever.

if i can dream

DREAMER

Elvis closed the '68 special with a new song written just for the show, "If I Can Dream," with lyrics based on the composer's conversations with the King. Through "If I Can Dream," Elvis expressed his feelings about life and about his hopes for the future. It's one of the few songs the King ever sang that contained a message—a message which is still clear and true.

ELVIS: THE KING OF ROCK & ROLL

8

"Presley remains a true American artist—one of the greatest in American popular music, a singer of native brilliance and a performer of magnetic dimensions."

—Jim Millar, *Rolling Stone*

The Concert Years

The World's Greatest Entertainer

After the huge success of the '68 special, Elvis was more in demand than ever. On July 31, 1969, billed as "The World's Greatest Entertainer," he opened his first gig in Las Vegas since 1956. The sold-out show at the International Hotel was met with ecstatic approval—whistles, shouts, deafening applause, and more than one standing ovation—and the four-week engagement broke all attendance records.

On The Road Again

Tired of Hollywood and feeling out of touch with his audience, Elvis returned to the concert circuit and never looked back. Known as the "concert years," 1969 through 1977 saw nearly 1,100 live performances. Four sold-out shows at New York's Madison Square Garden in 1972 were attended by no less than John Lennon, George Harrison, Bob Dylan, David Bowie, and Art Garfunkel. The 1973 TV special, "Elvis—Aloha from Hawaii"—beamed live across the Pacific and shown taped in America and Europe—was seen by over a billion people in forty countries.

my way

FINAL BOW

Elvis Presley gave his last concert on June 26, 1977 in Indianapolis, Indiana. He was hospitalized that night, complaining of stomach troubles and muscle pain, but returned to Memphis the next day. During the next few weeks, between bouts of illness, he took Lisa Marie to an amusement park, played racquetball, and went to see *The Spy Who Loved Me*. On August 16, 1977, the King of Rock and Roll was found dead at Graceland.

Even before the King's untimely death in 1977, his image (and name) could be found throughout the world—on anything from pocket calendars to clothes, costume jewelry, and dolls. The incredible and wildly successful avalanche of merchandise left his fans literally mesmerized, and today an increasing number of fans and collectors avidly seek out Elvis memorabilia. After years of lobbying, the U. S. Postal Service got in on the action with the Elvis stamp, issued on what would have been Elvis' fifty-eighth birthday—January 8, 1993.

"I'm not king. Christ is king. I'm just a singer."
—Elvis

The Collectible Elvis

Gotta Have It!

Elvis' popularity has never dimmed, and neither has the demand for mementos of his life. Memorabilia is available in all-Elvis shops, through catalogues, at flea and antique markets, even over the Internet. Elvisiana is a billion-dollar industry.

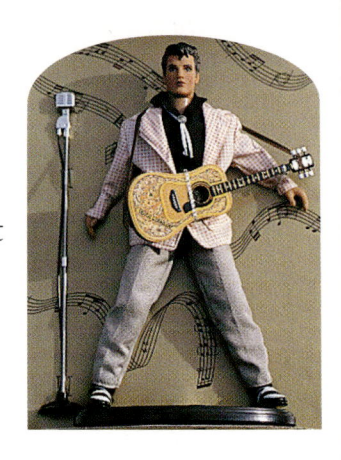

Sold to the Highest . . .

In November of 1996, the last of the Elvis Presley Museum Collection was auctioned at Butterfield & Butterfield's Los Angeles gallery, netting over $380,000. At a 1994 auction, one of Elvis' jumpsuits fetched a whopping $68,500 and a pair of his sunglasses brought in over $26,000. But other mementos, less personal but no less treasured, go for more reasonable sums. Menus from Elvis' Las Vegas appearances, for instance, are usually priced from $30 to $150. And an adorable 1956 charm bracelet—featuring a framed photo of Elvis, a hound dog, a guitar, and a heart inscribed with the words "heart break"—costs about $225. Of course, new Elvisiana is still being manufactured by numerous companies, much to the delight of fans and collectors alike.

ELVIS PRESLEY – ROCK AND ROLL LEGEND

15TH ANNIVERSARY OF HIS DEATH

Elvis stamps are truly an international phenomenon.

A collectible moment: President Nixon with the King in the Oval Office.

Things go better with Elvis! At this diner, an Elvis statuette competes for display space with a tabletop jukebox.

"Elvis is my man!"
—JANIS JOPLIN

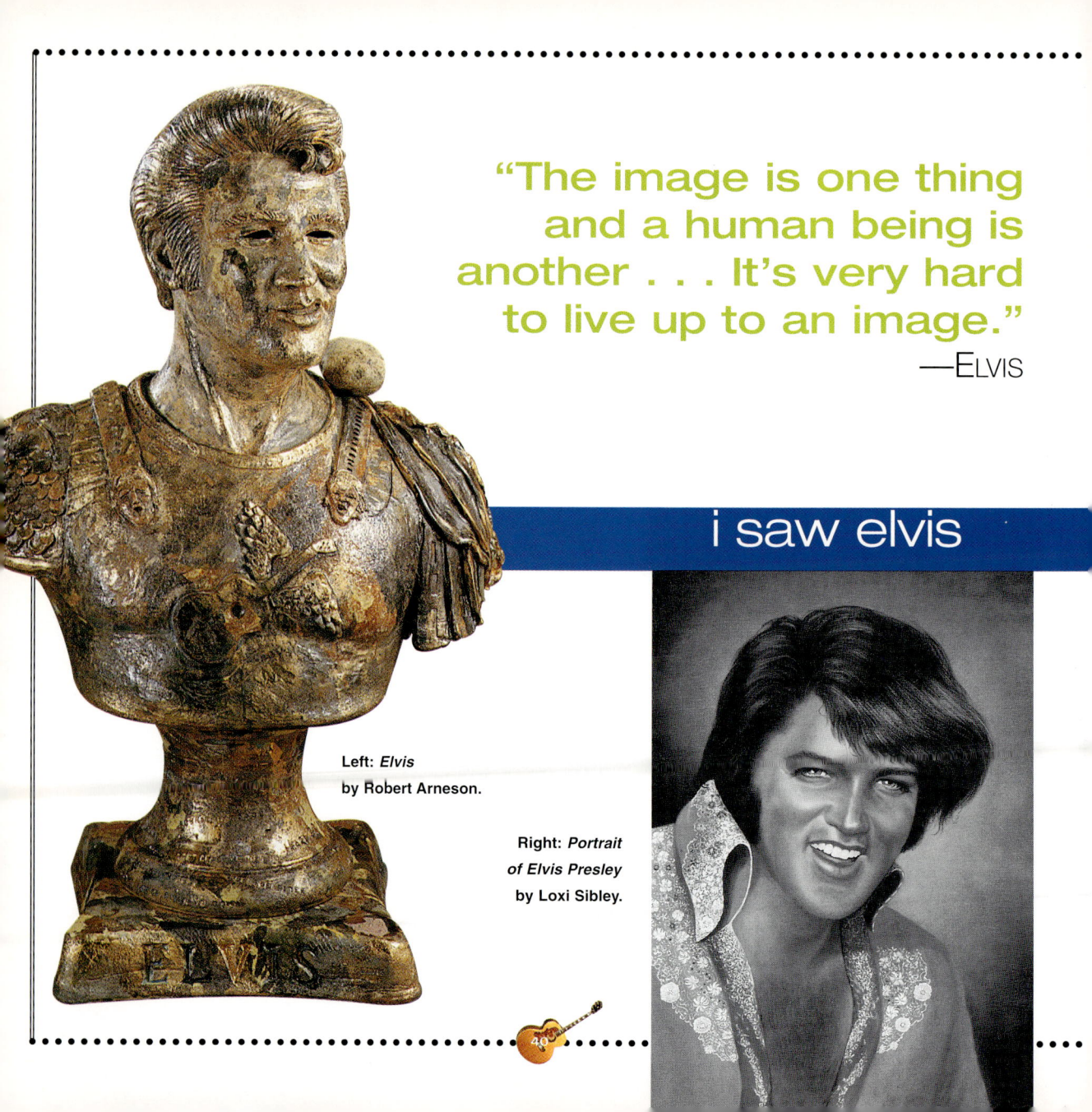

"The image is one thing and a human being is another . . . It's very hard to live up to an image."
—Elvis

i saw elvis

Left: *Elvis* by Robert Arneson.

Right: *Portrait of Elvis Presley* by Loxi Sibley.

···· ELVIS: THE KING OF ROCK & ROLL ····

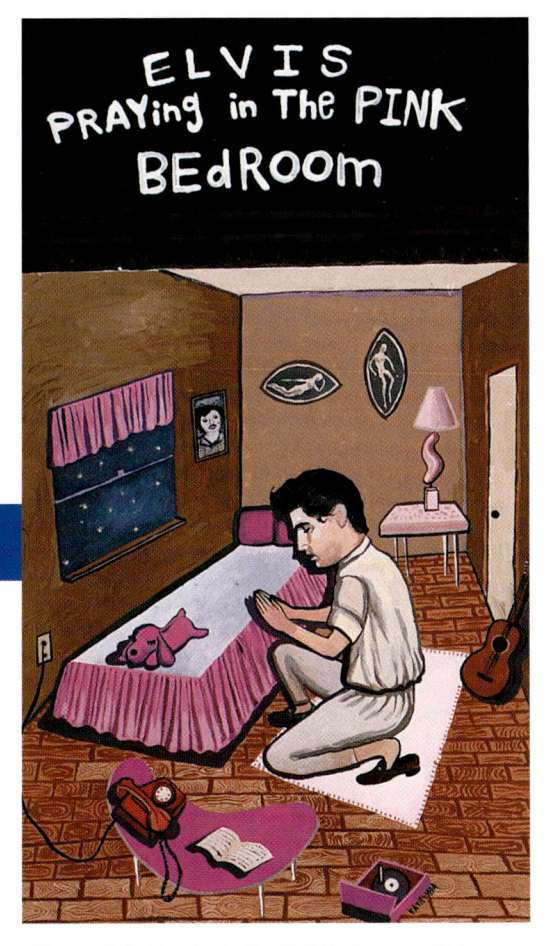

Above: *Elvis Praying in the Pink Bedroom* by Kata Billups; top right: *I Saw Elvis at the Playboy Club* by Kata Billups; bottom right: *Elvis Presley at the McDonalds* by Kata Billups.

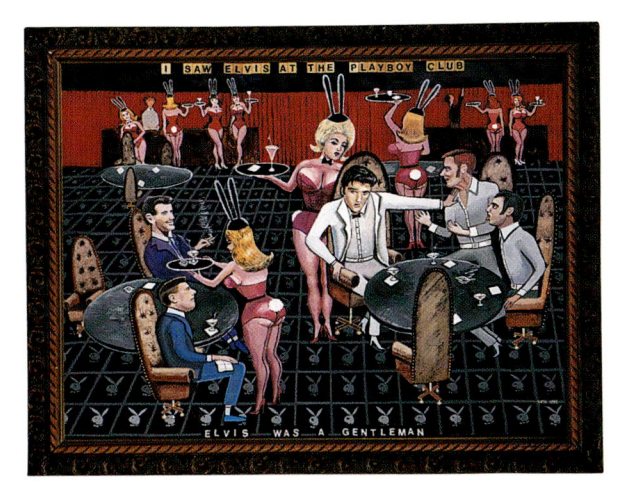

CAN YOU SPOT THE REAL ELVIS?

After Elvis' death, someone decided to perform shows dressed as Elvis, and the phenomenon spread like wildfire. Today, dozens of men (and a few women and children) make a living being "Elvis." Whether they're called Elvis impersonators, Elvis tribute artists, or Elvis stylists, all, in their own way, are living glorifications of the King.

> "I grew my hair like him and imitated his stage act."
> —Paul Simon

1. Norm Jones 2. Dave Carlson
3. El Vez 4. Brendan Paul
5. Elvis Presley 6. Trent Carlini

NEW YORK LOVES ELVIS

MAY THE KING REST IN PEACE
ELVIS
ELVIS PRESLEY
JANUARY 8, 1935 - AUGUST 16, 1977
DEL VIKINGS

ELVIS
I LOVE YOU
TATE
VICKIE
11-27-93
ELVIS WE'LL HAVE A BLUE CHRISTMAS WITHOUT YOU!
LOVE YOU
SANTANA
"POOPIE"
ELVIS, you
RE IN OUR
ARTS, FOREVER
Love Always
OUR FRIENDS
OM WEST VIRGINIA
August 1994
ELVIS 17 YEARS And Still Loving You! DAWN-DON
ELVIS ALWAYS ON OUR MIND FOREVER IN OUR HEART
TO ELVIS LOVE SHANNON
ELVIS MY HAPPINESS
FRANCE 8.16.94
LISA

ELVIS: THE KING OF ROCK & ROLL

ELVIS REMEMBERED

SAINT ELVIS

Some people pay homage to the King not at a museum, but in a chapel or shrine. Portland, Oregon's 24-hour Church of Elvis, part of the Where's the Art! gallery, offers a coin-operated display, photo-ops, and weddings. Students at the Massachusetts Institute of Technology have erected their own shrine dedicated to Elvis. Not to be left out, Las Vegas has the Graceland Wedding Chapel, where Elvis' marriage license hangs on the wall and Elvis impersonators serenade fans lucky enough to be married there.

The opposite page shows (top left, clockwise) the Presley family graves at Graceland, graffiti from the Graceland wall, and a tribute to the King after his death.

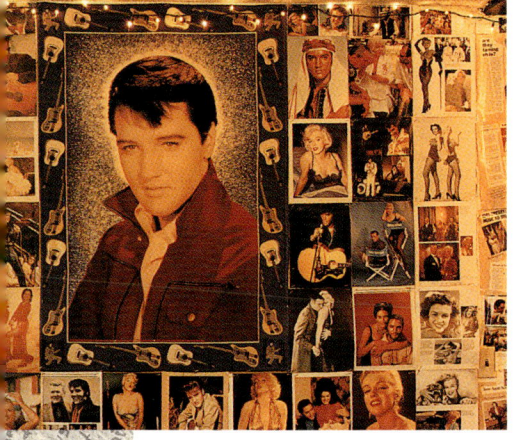

The Candlelight Vigil

Each year, from August 9th to the 17th, the anniversary of the King's death, Graceland celebrates Elvis Week. Fans converge from all over the world to reminisce and take part in myriad special events, including concerts, panel discussions, dance parties, and dinners. But the highlight of the week is the Candlelight Vigil, when thousands gather outside the Music Gate at dusk, then proceed, carrying lit candles, in hushed single-file to the Meditation Garden to pay their respects at Elvis' grave.

"Long after I'm gone, what I did today will be heard by someone. I just want them to get the best of what I had."
—Elvis

PHOTO CREDITS

Kata Billups, Mount Pleasant, SC 41 (left, top & bottom right)

Dave Carlson Productions 42 (right)

City of Ottawa Archives, Andrews Newton Collection 3

Graceland Wedding Chapel, Las Vegas 42 (left), 43 (bottom left)

Hirshhorn Museum and Sculpture Garden, Smithsonian Institution, Gift of the Sydney & Frances Lewis Foundation, 1985 40 (left)

Henry Horenstein 26

KK Productions 38 (top & bottom)

The Kobal Collection 6 (bottom), 8 (left), 10, 15, 16 (top & bottom), 19 (left, top right, bottom right), 30, 31 (bottom left & right), 35 (left & right)

Dan Lentino Management 43 (right)

Jim Markham 44 (top left)

Patti McConville & Les Sumner 36–37, 38 (top left)

Laura A. McElroy 28–29

Neutrogena Corp. 24 (top right)

Richard Nixon Library & Birthplace 39 (background & bottom right)

Michael Ochs Archives 1, 4 (right), 5 (top), 7 (left), 9 (bottom right), 11 (left & top right), 13 (bottom left), 14 (right), 17 (top), 20 (right), 21 (left), 24 (top left), 27, 32 (top), 34

Photofest 5 (bottom), 6 (top left), 8 (top), 9 (top), 11 (bottom right), 12, 13 (top left & bottom right), 14 (left), 17 (bottom), 18, 20 (left), 21 (right), 22 (top & bottom), 31 (top), 32 (bottom)

Photographers/Aspen

Tony Demin 45 (right)

The Picture Cube

David Ball 44 (right)

Rodger Kingston 39 (bottom)

Eric Roth 40 (bottom), 44 (bottom left)

Picture Perfect 25 (top right & bottom)

Popshots, Inc. 36 (bottom right)

Private collection 6 (top right), 7 (right), 9 (bottom left), 23, 33, 43 (center)

Shooting Star 24 (bottom), 25 (top left)

Stellartists 43 (top left)

Unicorn Stock Photo

Florent Flipper 46–47

Scott Liles 4 (left)

Aneal Vohra 45 (left)

Additional copyright information:

Pop-up greeting card (page 38) ©Popshots, Inc., Westport, CT ©Elvis Presley Enterprises, Inc.

Elvis stamp potholders (page 38), stamp design ©U.S. Postal Service ©Elvis Presley Enterprises, Inc.